P9-DOC-379

Biographies

Harriet Tubman

Conductor to Freedom

by Nick Healy

Consultant:
Lois Brown, PhD
Museum of Afro-American History
Boston, Massachusetts

Capstone
press

Mankato, Minnesota

EAST CHICAGO PUBLIC LIBRARY
EAST CHICAGO, INDIANA

RAP 867 5375

Fact Finders is published by Capstone Press,
151 Good Counsel Drive, P.O. Box 669, Mankato, Minnesota 56002.
www.capstonepress.com

Copyright © 2005 by Capstone Press. All rights reserved.
No part of this publication may be reproduced in whole or in part, or stored in a retrieval
system, or transmitted in any form or by any means, electronic, mechanical, photocopying,
recording, or otherwise, without written permission of the publisher.
For information regarding permission, write to Capstone Press,
151 Good Counsel Drive, P.O. Box 669, Dept. R, Mankato, Minnesota 56002.
Printed in the United States of America

Library of Congress Cataloging-in-Publication Data
Healy, Nick.
    Harriet Tubman: conductor to freedom / by Nick Healy.
    p. cm.—(Fact finders. Biographies)
    Includes bibliographical references and index.
    ISBN 0-7368-3743-4 (hardcover)
    ISBN 0-7368-5186-0 (paperback)
    1. Tubman, Harriet, 1820?–1913—Juvenile literature. 2. Slaves—United States—
Biography—Juvenile literature. 3. African American women—Biography—Juvenile
literature. 4. African Americans—Biography—Juvenile literature. 5. Underground
railroad—Juvenile literature. I. Title. II. Series.
E444.T82H43 2005
973.7'115'092—dc22
                                                              2004009815

Summary: A brief introduction to the life of Harriet Tubman, who spoke out against slavery
    in the United States and saved hundreds of African Americans by leading them north
    on the Underground Railroad.

Editorial Credits
Donald Lemke, editor; Juliette Peters, set designer; Patrick D. Dentinger, book designer and
    illustrator; Kelly Garvin, photo researcher; Scott Thoms, photo editor

Photo Credits
Collection of the Cayuga Museum of History and Art, 19; Corbis/Bettmann, 18; Corbis/Lee
Snider, 25; Courtesy of the Caroline County Historical Society, Denton, Maryland, 7, 14;
Getty Images Inc./Hulton Archive, 21; Getty Images Inc./Time & Life Pictures, 17; The
Granger Collection, New York, cover; "Harriet Tubman's Underground Railroad" by
international acclaimed artist Paul Collins, Paul Collins Fine Art, Michigan, 5; Janice
Northcutt Huse, Artist, Port Charlotte, FL, 11, 12–13, 15; Library of Congress, 26; The New
York Public Library, Schomburg Center, 1, 9, 23, 27

1 2 3 4 5 6 10 09 08 07 06 05

J
973.7092
HEA

Table of Contents

Chapter 1

Crossing Over

A young woman hurried along a riverbank with two men. The men were running from a life of **slavery**. The woman was leading them to a place where slavery was against the law. If caught, they would be punished or killed.

Suddenly, the woman stopped. She sensed danger ahead. She turned and whispered to the runaway slaves. They must cross the river, she said.

The river was cold and deep. The men were not sure they could make it. The woman didn't listen. She stared ahead and stepped into the icy water. The men followed her. They didn't know what else to do.

Harriet Tubman leads runaway slaves to freedom in this painting by artist Paul Collins.

The woman kept moving forward into deeper water. Finally, the group reached the other side. Harriet Tubman had led the men safely across the river. They were on their way to freedom.

Chapter 2

Born into Slavery

Harriet Tubman was born around 1820. Her parents were Benjamin and Harriet Ross. They were slaves in Dorchester County, Maryland. Slaves were the property of their owners. Many African Americans lived as slaves in the United States.

Tubman started working when she was about 5 years old. A neighbor named Miss Susan wanted a slave to care for her baby. Edward Brodess, who owned Tubman, sent her to do the job.

Miss Susan made Tubman care for her baby all day and night. If the baby cried, Tubman was punished. Miss Susan often beat Tubman with a whip.

Tubman grew up in a small home similar to this Maryland slave cabin.

Miss Susan was not happy with Tubman. She sent her back to Brodess. He decided Tubman was not good at housework. He sent her to work outdoors. Soon, young Tubman was picking crops and chopping wood with grown men.

A Terrible Injury

As a teenager, Tubman continued to work for other people. One fall, Tubman's owner sent her to work for a man named Barrett. He owned a nearby farm.

While working for Barrett, Tubman watched another slave sneak away from the fields. The slave headed for a nearby town. Tubman saw an **overseer** go after the slave with a whip. She followed them.

The overseer cornered the runaway slave inside a local store. As the slave tried to escape, the overseer ordered Tubman to help catch him. She would not.

FACT!

At birth, Tubman was named Araminta Ross. Later, she honored her family by taking her mother's first name.

▲ Southern slaves
often planted and
harvested crops
for their owners.

Instead, Tubman stepped between
the men, blocking the overseer. In his
anger, the overseer threw an iron weight
at the runaway slave. It missed him and
hit Tubman's head.

Tubman spent months in bed. Her
family helped her get better. Tubman's
forehead was scarred forever. She also
had headaches and fainting spells the
rest of her life.

Chapter 3

Escape to Freedom

Tubman married in 1844. Her husband, John Tubman, came from the same county in Maryland. He was a free African American. Even though Tubman married a free man, she remained a slave.

Tubman often talked to her husband about running away. Maryland was only 90 miles (145 kilometers) from Pennsylvania. Slavery was against the law in Pennsylvania. John did not want to go. He thought trying to escape was too dangerous.

In this painting by Janice Northcutt Huse, Tubman talks to her husband about running away.

In 1849, Tubman's owner died. Tubman was not sure what would happen next. A new owner could take her south, farther away from freedom. She could also be torn from her husband, mother, and other relatives.

Tubman did not wait to find out what would happen. In September 1849, she decided to head for Pennsylvania alone.

On the Run

The journey to freedom was dangerous. Tubman traveled only at night. It was too risky to move during the day. If caught, she could be killed.

People who helped runaway slaves could be punished. Luckily, Tubman knew a brave white woman who helped her. The woman gave Tubman a piece of paper. It had the names of families who would give Tubman food or a place to hide. These people were part of the **Underground Railroad**.

FACT!

Tubman was a short woman. She stood only 5 feet (1.5 meters) tall.

◄ Tubman heads for Pennsylvania in this Janice Northcutt Huse painting.

The Underground Railroad

The Underground Railroad was not a real railroad. It was a system of helpful people and safe places for runaway slaves. People who worked on the Underground Railroad were called **conductors**. They helped slaves sneak away to freedom in the northern states. Each stop along the Underground Railroad was called a **station**.

Some historians believe Tubman got help at this Maryland home on the first night of her escape.

During her escape, Tubman got help from conductors on the Underground Railroad. But the journey was still difficult. Tubman often walked as many as 10 miles (16 kilometers) each night. She followed rivers and trails in the dark. She walked out of Maryland and through Delaware. After weeks of danger, Tubman arrived in Philadelphia, Pennsylvania. She was finally free.

⬆ In this scene imagined by artist Janice Northcutt Huse, a woman on the Underground Railroad finds Tubman a place to hide.

QUOTE

"I had crossed the line of which I had so long been dreaming. I was free."
—Harriet Tubman

Chapter 4

Conductor on the Railroad

Once in Pennsylvania, Tubman got a job and worked hard. She also wanted to help others escape slavery. Tubman became a conductor on the Underground Railroad.

Tubman's First Rescue

Tubman's first trip back to Maryland was in 1850. She went to rescue her niece Keziah. Keziah was married to a free African American named John Bowley. They had two children. Tubman met Keziah and her family in Baltimore, Maryland. She helped guide them to Pennsylvania.

Tubman posed for this portrait in 1855. It is the earliest photograph of her.

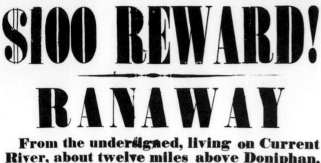

Slave owners offered rewards for the capture of runaway slaves.

Tubman's first trip was a success. Within months, she returned to the South and rescued more people. She also tried to get her husband to move north. But John had married another woman and did not want to leave.

New Dangers

Around the same time, the Fugitive Slave Act of 1793 was changed. Even free states became unsafe for runaway slaves. Changes in the law allowed owners to hunt for slaves anywhere in the United States. Canada became the only safe place for runaway slaves.

Tubman now had to bring slaves all the way from Maryland to Canada. The journey was more than 500 miles (805 kilometers).

During the 1850s, Tubman and most of her family settled in St. Catherines, Ontario. Tubman brought her parents north in 1857.

Tubman led people to freedom on the Underground Railroad until 1860. She made 19 trips into Maryland and other slave states. She brought at least 300 people to freedom in the northern United States and Canada.

QUOTE

"I can say what most conductors can't say, I never ran my train off the tracks and I never lost a passenger."
—Harriet Tubman

Tubman often dressed up for her portraits.

Chapter 5

Tubman Goes to War

In the 1860s, slavery had divided the nation. Most people in Northern states wanted slavery to end. Many Southerners wanted the right to keep slaves. This debate helped lead to the Civil War (1861–1865).

A Nurse for the North

Tubman signed up to be a nurse for the Union army in the North. She knew how to make medicine from plants and roots. She cared for many sick and injured soldiers.

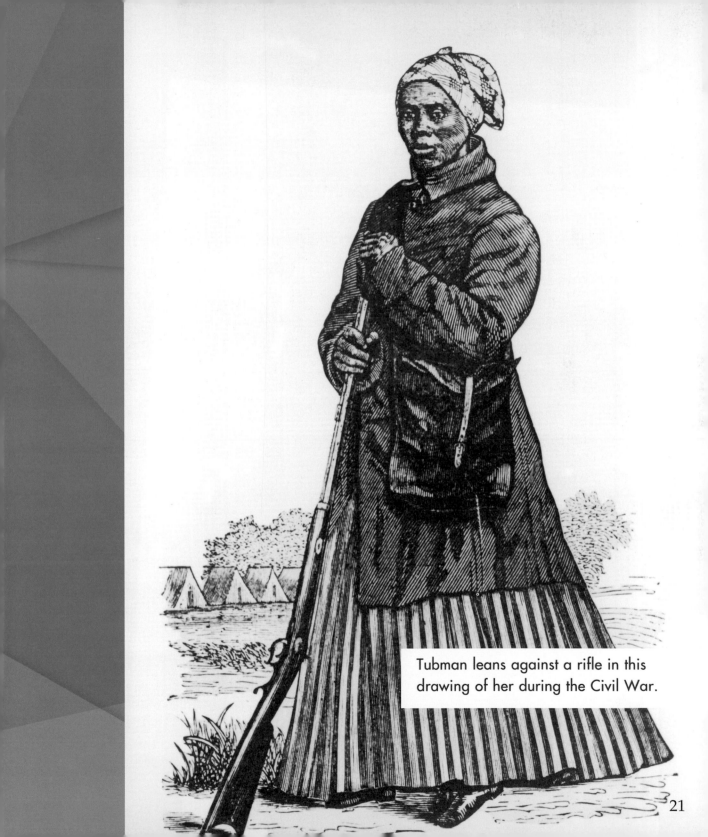

Tubman leans against a rifle in this drawing of her during the Civil War.

QUOTE

"We saw lightning and that was the guns; and then we heard thunder and that was the big guns; and then we heard the rain falling and that was the blood falling."
—Harriet Tubman, describing her work as a Civil War spy

Union Leader

Tubman also became a spy and a scout. She often pretended to be a slave in order to slip across enemy lines. While there, she found out many things about the Confederate army in the South. In 1863, Tubman led the Combahee River Raid in South Carolina. She guided 150 soldiers and freed 750 slaves in one night.

The Union army freed many slaves during the war. Many of them were wounded or sick. Their clothes were like rags. Their stomachs were empty. Tubman cared for them.

▲ After the war,
Tubman (left)
settled in Auburn,
New York, with
friends and family.

In April 1865, the North defeated
the South, and the war finally ended.
In December, **Congress** passed the
13th Amendment. This addition to
the U.S. Constitution ended slavery
in the United States.

Chapter 6

Working for Others

After the war, Tubman went to Auburn, New York. Her parents had moved there too. They were growing old. Tubman took care of her parents until they died.

The Harriet Tubman Home

Like many former slaves, Tubman had little money. The U.S. government owed Tubman money for her work during the Civil War. But the money never came.

In 1869, Tubman married a man named Nelson Davis. He had fought for the Union army during the war. Davis died in 1888. Tubman later received a widow's **pension** of $8 a month.

The Harriet Tubman Home in Auburn, New York, has been a memorial to Tubman's life since 1953.

For many years, Tubman dreamed of buying land next to her home. In 1908, she finally was able to buy 25 acres (10 hectares). Tubman opened a home for older and ill African Americans. It was called the Harriet Tubman Home.

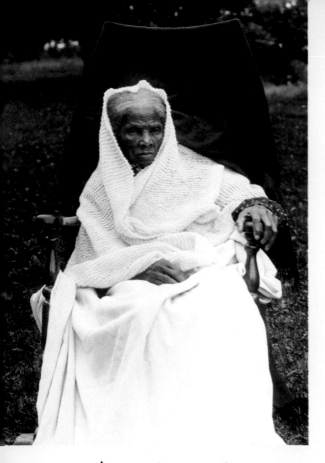

▲ Around 1910, Tubman posed for her last portrait.

Tubman kept fighting for what she believed. She spoke in favor of women's right to vote. She helped many former slaves. She also raised money for African American schools in the South.

In her final years, Tubman became a patient in the charity home she built. She lived there until her death on March 10, 1913.

Today, the Harriet Tubman Home is a museum. People from around the world visit it to learn about Tubman's courageous life.

Fast Facts

Full name: Harriet Tubman

Birth: About 1820

Death: March 10, 1913

Hometown: Dorchester County, Maryland

Parents: Benjamin and Harriet Ross

Siblings: 10 brothers and sisters

Husbands: John Tubman and Nelson Davis

Education: No formal education

Achievements:

> Brought about 300 enslaved people to freedom in the northern United States and Canada, 1851–1860
>
> Led Combahee River Raid, freeing about 750 slaves, 1863
>
> Started Harriet Tubman Home for African Americans living in New York, 1908

Time Line

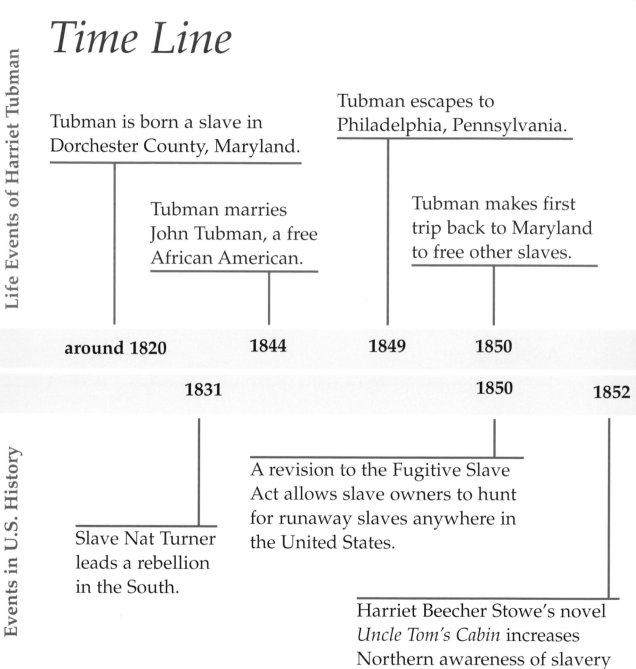

Life Events of Harriet Tubman

Tubman is born a slave in Dorchester County, Maryland.

Tubman marries John Tubman, a free African American.

Tubman escapes to Philadelphia, Pennsylvania.

Tubman makes first trip back to Maryland to free other slaves.

around 1820   1844   1849   1850

1831   1850   1852

Events in U.S. History

Slave Nat Turner leads a rebellion in the South.

A revision to the Fugitive Slave Act allows slave owners to hunt for runaway slaves anywhere in the United States.

Harriet Beecher Stowe's novel *Uncle Tom's Cabin* increases Northern awareness of slavery and the Underground Railroad.

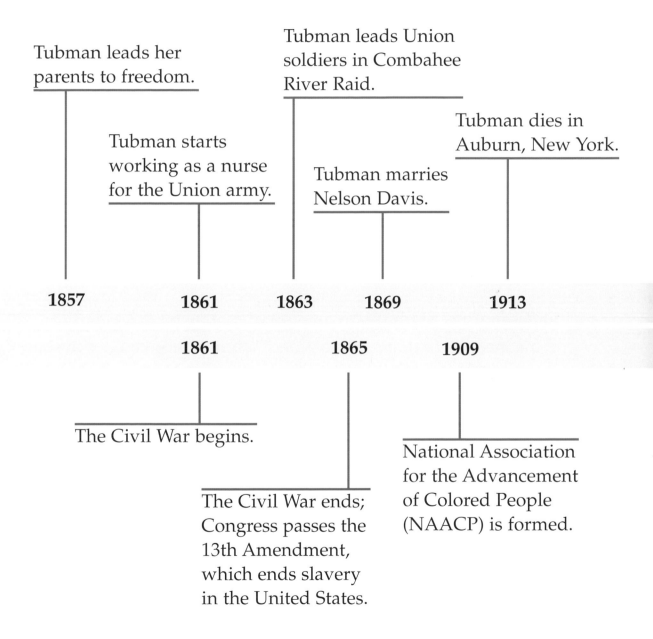

Tubman leads her parents to freedom.

Tubman leads Union soldiers in Combahee River Raid.

Tubman dies in Auburn, New York.

Tubman starts working as a nurse for the Union army.

Tubman marries Nelson Davis.

1857   1861   1863   1869   1913

1861   1865   1909

The Civil War begins.

The Civil War ends; Congress passes the 13th Amendment, which ends slavery in the United States.

National Association for the Advancement of Colored People (NAACP) is formed.

Glossary

conductor (kuhn-DUK-tur)—a person who helped runaway slaves on the Underground Railroad

Congress (KONG-griss)—the government body of the United States that makes laws, made up of the Senate and the House of Representatives

overseer (OH-vur-see-uhr)—a person in charge of watching and punishing slaves

pension (PEN-shuhn)—an amount of money paid regularly to someone who is retired from work; Tubman received her husband's pension after he died.

slavery (SLAY-vur-ee)—the owning of other people; slaves are forced to work without pay.

station (STAY-shuhn)—a hiding place on the Underground Railroad

Underground Railroad (UHN-dur-ground RAYL-rohd)—a system of helpful people and safe places for runaway slaves during the mid-1800s

Internet Sites

FactHound offers a safe, fun way to find Internet sites related to this book. All of the sites on FactHound have been researched by our staff.

Here's how:

1. Visit *www.facthound.com*
2. Type in this special code **0736837434** for age-appropriate sites. Or enter a search word related to this book for a more general search.
3. Click on the **Fetch It** button.

FactHound will fetch the best sites for you!

Read More

Klingel, Cynthia Fitterer. *Harriet Tubman: Abolitionist and Underground Railroad Conductor.* Our People. Chanhassen, Minn.: Child's World, 2004.

Martin, Michael. *Harriet Tubman and the Underground Railroad.* Graphic Library. Graphic History. Mankato, Minn.: Capstone Press, 2005.

Weidt, Maryann N. *Harriet Tubman.* History Maker Bios. Minneapolis: Lerner, 2003.

Index